When Business Becomes Heavy

Letting Go of Hustle, Embracing God's Pace,
and Building a Business That Doesn't Break

Andrea Russell

ISBN: 978-1-971349-17-6

Table of Contents

Introduction

You're not failing. You're just carrying what God didn't assign.

Have you ever felt like you were doing "all the right things" in business... and yet nothing felt right?

Like you were building, posting, praying, tithing, serving, launching, and still the numbers weren't adding up, and the peace wasn't showing up?

That was me. Smiling in Zoom calls, quoting Scripture on Instagram, doing everything "faith + works" told me to do... but quietly wondering why my soul felt like it was breaking while I tried to build.

Here's the truth I had to learn the hard way:

Just because it's good doesn't mean it's God.

And just because you're gifted doesn't mean you're supposed to carry every assignment that comes your way.

We've glamorized grinding and baptized burnout and called it "purpose."

We've overbooked our calendars, overextended our budgets, and underestimated the power of stillness.

But I want to say something to you that I wish someone had said to me back then:

You're not behind. You're just untrained.

You weren't born knowing how to build a business God's way. Nobody handed you a spiritual operations manual with your LLC. That doesn't make you broken. It makes you ready.

This book isn't about striving. It's not a 7-step blueprint to become a six-figure Christian. It's not a motivational pep talk or a performance manual.

This is a reminder.

A wake-up call.

A personal permission slip to lay the pressure down and pick up peace.

Inside, I'll share what God taught me when I was exhausted, overworked, and on the brink of quitting everything, even the "God things."

You'll learn how to:

Discern the difference between Kingdom assignments and Christian ambition.

Trade burnout for overflow.

Let the Holy Spirit co-lead your business.

Make profit without guilt.

And rest without shame.

Matthew 11:28-30 says it best:

"Come to Me, all who are weary and burdened, and I will give you rest. Take My yoke upon you... For My yoke is easy, and My burden is light."

If business has felt heavy, friend, this is your confirmation:

God never meant for you to carry it alone.

Let's trade pressure for purpose.

Let's S.O.A.R.

CHAPTER 1

Trading Pressure for Purpose

Let's be real, business isn't always cupcakes and clients winning.

There are days when the to-do list looks like a scroll from the Old Testament. Days when the sales aren't coming in, the family doesn't understand, and the pressure feels suffocating.

And as a Christian woman entrepreneur, it's even heavier. Because not only are you carrying the weight of your business, but you're also trying to do it God's way.

If you've ever felt like building your business is making you crumble, you're not alone.

God never asked you to hustle yourself into burnout.

This chapter is for the woman who loves God and loves her business but is tired of the pressure and ready to build with peace. Let's trade the grind for grace and unpack what it really means to work *with* God instead of *for* Him.

The Turning Point: From Breakdown to Breakthrough

Let me tell you what I've learned the hard way: You cannot build a business on burned-out fumes and call it faith.

There was a season I thought crying in the shower, clinging to Scripture with one hand and QuickBooks with the other, was just how a "faithful entrepreneur" operated. I kept telling myself, "This is just warfare... I have to push through."

But God didn't call me to strive. He called me to abide.

"Come to me, all you who are weary and burdened, and I will give you rest." - Matthew 11:28

That verse isn't just about naps, lovely. It's about partnership. About not carrying what was never meant to be yours alone. I had to learn that being "faithful" didn't mean being frantic.

It meant making room for God in the daily operations of my business.

Not just inviting Him into the marketing plan, but also the Monday meetings.

Not just praying over launches, but over client boundaries and invoice reminders.

Not just quoting Proverbs 31, but living like a woman who trusts her God to sustain the work of her hands.

This was the shift.

It wasn't about quitting. It was about rebuilding from alignment.

3 Signs Your Business is Out of Alignment

Now, let's get real practical. Because sometimes, we spiritualize struggle and call it a season when really, it's a signal.

Here are three signs your business is running on pressure, not purpose:

- Sign #1: You're constantly anxious, even when things are "working."

  You hit your revenue goal, but your peace still hasn't shown up. That's not growth; that's hustle wearing a Jesus tee.

- Sign #2: You're doing everything alone.

  You pray, but don't delegate. You believe God can multiply, but you won't trust Him enough to hire help. Isolation is not a fruit of the Spirit.

- Sign #3: You avoid reviewing your finances.

You'd rather binge a podcast on faith + biz than open your Stripe account. But clarity is kindness. Stewardship requires attention, not avoidance.

If you nodded at any of these, you're not broken. You're just misaligned. And misalignment doesn't mean failure. It means you have an opportunity to recalibrate with the Holy Spirit.

The S.O.A.R. Method: A Kingdom Reframe

When I created my signature program, S.O.A.R., it wasn't about giving women a 5-step hustle plan. It was about giving them a faith-based framework to build a business that breathes, one that honors their season, their story, and their Savior.

Let me break it down real quick:

S - Surrender what's not from God (especially the stuff that looks good but isn't fruitful).

O - Overcome the lies of hustle culture and lack-driven thinking.

A - Align with biblical principles of stewardship, rest, and wisdom.

R - Rise into the profitable, purpose-driven woman God created you to be.

This method doesn't just help women stop striving; it helps them build in alignment. Businesses that scale without stress. Strategies rooted in kingdom wisdom, not marketing trends.

God is Not a Hustle Coach

One of the hardest things I had to "unlearn" was this: God isn't clapping because I'm exhausted.

He's not impressed with my 18-hour days.

He's not keeping score based on my DM reply time.

And He's definitely not sitting up in Heaven going, "Yes, girl! You only slept four hours and still posted on IG before sunrise!"

No.

God is a good Father. Not a hustle coach. Not a CEO whispering pressure over your shoulder.

He delights when you rest, trust, and operate in wisdom. That's why when business feels heavy, it's often a spiritual cue to pause and ask:

"Lord, what part of this load did I pick up without You?"

From Heavy to Holy

My lovely sister, your business was never supposed to break you.

Yes, there will be hard days.

Yes, there will be stretching seasons.

But God never designed your assignment to crush you.

He designed it to refine you.

To deepen your trust.

To mature your stewardship.

To reflect His goodness in every client call, product sale, and financial breakthrough.

So if business feels heavy right now, take a breath.

You're not failing. You're growing.

You're not behind. You're becoming.

You're not too late. You're just stepping into alignment.

And on the other side of that alignment?

Peace that doesn't make sense.

Provision that doesn't run dry.

Purpose that doesn't burn you out.

Are you ready?

Let's trade pressure for purpose.

Reflection Questions (Let's Go Deeper)

I want to challenge you to sit with these questions in prayer and journaling:

1. When did your business first start to feel heavy, not holy?
2. Have you ever confused hustle with faithfulness? What did that look like?
3. What areas of your life or business are you still trying to control instead of surrendering?
4. How has striving shown up in your thoughts, schedule, or decision-making lately?
5. Reset Exercise: Take 10 quiet minutes to journal, "Lord, what pressure have I picked up that You never assigned to me?" Write whatever comes.

Chapter Summary

So many Christian women in business face silent struggles in their business when they carry their business on their shoulders instead of surrendering it to the Lord. This struggle is real, and it reminds us that even good work becomes rather heavy when we move ahead of the Lord's pace. It's okay to feel tired; you're not weak. You are only human. But the good news is that with God, you were never meant to carry it all alone. Let this be a reminder to cast your cares on him, for he cares for you (**1 Peter 5:7**).

In the next chapter, we will explore what it means to learn the lesson of trusting this Lord with your assignment.

CHAPTER 2

Learning to Trust the Assignment

Do you ever feel like God called the wrong person? Like, he must've meant someone else?

Someone more qualified, more educated, more polished, more... Not you?

That was me. I had no MBA. I did grow up in a family of business moguls. I was a divorced mom with three kids, a pantry of Dollar Store snacks, and a prayer life that often sounded like,

"Lord, are you sure about this?"

But here's what I've learned: God doesn't call the already qualified. He qualifies the call. And sometimes the only qualification you need is a 'yes' that's louder than your fear.

Your 'Not Qualified' Moment

If you've ever thought, 'I can't do this business thing. I don't have the background. I'm not good with numbers. I don't even know how to market myself.'

Welcome.

You're in good company. Many people have experienced that.

We've been fed this lie that business is for the bold, the polished, and the already successful.

But God loves using the least likely. That's His favorite strategy.

Remember Moses? Couldn't speak clearly.

Gideon? Hiding in the winepress.

David? A shepherd boy.

If you've got a mustard seed of faith and a willingness to obey, you're more than qualified in God's eyes.

Obedience Over Clarity

One of the hardest parts of business, especially as a Christian woman, is saying 'yes' before the full picture is clear.

I used to ask God for a blueprint. He gave me a breadcrumb.

Starting my business felt like stepping out of the boat with zero swimming lessons.

But God kept showing up in unexpected ways. A check in the mail. A client referral I didn't ask for. Strength I didn't think I had at 3 a.m. when my kids were younger, and I still had to finish my clients' books.

Sometimes you don't need to see the whole staircase. You just need to take the next step.

Worldly Credentials vs God's Calling

The world will tell you that you need the letters, the likes, and the LinkedIn clout.

But God isn't moved by your resumé. He's moved by your obedience.

1 Corinthians 1:27 says, "God chose the foolish things of the world to shame the wise."

If He calls you, He'll equip you. That's not just spiritual fluff; that's a promise.

I recall the Lord telling me to relocate to the US as a single mom with three small kids. I thought he must have been joking. I had no green card or family to get me papers. But God turned my world upside down. I fasted and prayed, and in 30 days I had a work permit and did what he told me to do.

I truly believe that every time you show up in faith, heaven backs you up.

Lessons Learned in the Fire

Everything I know now? I learned by doing. Not dreaming. You don't gain Kingdom wisdom sitting in fear; you get it by walking with God through the unknown.

I didn't know how to set up systems. I learned. I didn't know how to price my services. I asked for help. I didn't know how to manage the cash flow. I trusted God and followed His lead. Every gap in my knowledge became an opportunity for growth.

Reflection Questions (Let's Go Deeper)

1. What assignment has God given you that you've tried to sidestep or delay?
2. Have you been confusing clarity with confirmation?
3. In what ways has fear of not being "qualified" slowed down your obedience?
4. How can you reframe risk as part of your walk with God, not a warning sign?
5. Reset Exercise: Make a list of things God has brought you through. Remind yourself of His track record.

Chapter Summary

Trying to do everything on your own is the killer of business. I have tried to do that more times than I can count. Simply because I thought I knew better than anyone else how things should be done. I felt the time I took to sit here training someone, I could get it done so much faster and exactly how I wanted it. But what I realized was, the only thing that was doing to me was making me more and more frustrated and overwhelmed. My encouragement to you now is this: You don't need to have everything all figured out to move forward. God is the one who trains and equips. Let this chapter be your reminder that clarity often follows obedience, not the other way around. How about just doing as scripture says, be still, trust the Lord with your assignment. He has got you covered.

In Chapter 3, we will discuss what they didn't teach us in church and school that we wish they had.

What They Didn't Teach Us in Church or School

Let's be honest, there are some things Sunday School just didn't prepare us for. No shade to flannel boards and memory verses, but learning how to file taxes, market your services, or price your offer without sounding apologetic? That wasn't part of the curriculum. And school? They might've taught us how to square a number or label mitochondria, but budgeting like a Kingdom entrepreneur or knowing how to discern between a good idea and a God idea? Not a single worksheet in sight.

This chapter is all about filling in those gaps because many of us were handed a Bible and told to be humble but not taught how to steward that calling into a business that actually pays the bills.

Hosea 4:6 says, "My people are destroyed for lack of knowledge."

Not lack of hustle. Not lack of heart. Lack of knowledge.

Fear's Favorite Lie: "You're Not Ready"

Let's talk about that lie straight from the pit: "You're not ready."

You've heard it. I've heard it. And if we're being honest, we've believed it way too many times.

That voice will always pop up the moment you try to take a step in obedience.

You're sitting there minding your business, and the Holy Spirit nudges you to launch something new or finally finish that thing He told you to start a year ago.

And before you can even pull out your laptop, fear whispers, "But what if you mess this up? You don't even have your website done."

And just like that, you're back to scrolling Instagram for "motivation" **(aka procrastination with a purpose)**.

Let me set you free: Nobody ever feels fully ready.

Moses didn't.

Esther didn't.

Gideon sure didn't.

And I bet your favorite business coach didn't either.

The question isn't whether you're ready. The question is whether you're willing.

I've launched programs with a prayer and a Google Doc. I've recorded videos without makeup or a perfect script.

And every time I took a step of obedience, God met me there.

See, readiness isn't a feeling. It's a decision. And faith doesn't wait for perfection; it responds to instruction.

Scripture says in 2 Corinthians 12:9, "My grace is sufficient for you, for my power is made perfect in weakness."

That means even if you feel underqualified, overwhelmed, or underprepared, God isn't. And He chose you, not the version of you that finally has it all together.

Let's stop letting fear dress itself up as wisdom. Sometimes we call it "being responsible" or "doing more research" when it's really just fear saying, "Stay small where it feels safe."

But you weren't made for small. You were made for impact.

The 5 Pillars of a Profitable Purpose-Driven Business

So now that we've talked about fear, let's move into some real building blocks. I call them the 5 Pillars of a Profitable Purpose-Driven Business. These aren't magic formulas, but they are truths I've lived and walked out with my clients, and they've helped us move from overwhelmed to aligned.

1. Clarity

If you don't know what you do and who you help, your business will stay foggy and broken.

Clarity is Kingdom currency. Before God gave Adam a helper, He gave him an assignment.

You need to know your lane.

Ask yourself:

- What problem do I solve?
- Who am I called to serve?
- What results do I help people get?

2. Messaging

Even Jesus had a clear message. ***"Repent, for the Kingdom of Heaven is near"*** wasn't vague.

Your business needs that same boldness. Messaging isn't about cute captions. It's about clear communication that connects to the people you're called to serve.

Stop trying to sound like everybody else.

Start sounding like you are the version of you that knows what God said and isn't afraid to say it with love.

3. Systems

Listen. You can be Holy Spirit-led and still have a Google Sheet. In fact, you need one. Or a CRM. Or a scheduling tool. Why? Because you're not just building a side hustle; you're building something that can sustain others.

God is not a God of confusion. Systems create freedom. Stop trying to carry everything in your head. That's how burnout starts.

4. Stewardship

This one's a biggie. You can't pray for overflow and then mismanage what you already have. Stewardship is not just about your money; it's about your time, your clients, your message, and your capacity.

God promotes stewardship. And when you handle the little things well, He'll trust you more. *(See Matthew 25:21.)*

5. Accountability

Who are you walking with? Because isolation is a slow death for a purpose-driven entrepreneur. You need people who will call out your excuses, remind you what God said, and pull you out of pity parties when things feel hard.

This is why I created the S.O.A.R. framework.

Because most of us don't need more information, we need implementation.

And someone to walk with us as we rise.

Reflection Questions (Let's Go Deeper)

1. Have you been asking God to bless your plans or show you His?
2. What part of your business are you still gripping too tightly?
3. What are you afraid will happen if you really let go?

4. How do you define success and does your definition align with God's?

5. Reset Exercise: Write a surrender prayer. Be honest. Invite God into the very place you've been keeping Him out.

Chapter Summary

Fear is a killer of all things good, even though we didn't learn the right strategies at church or school to have a perfect business. One thing we have learned is that when we put our trust in the Lord, He will do what He does best, and that is turn all things around for the good of those who are called, according to His purpose, and who love Him (**Romans 8:28**).

We don't need to know every detail perfectly, because God does. Lay down the hustle-build blueprint and pick up the Spirit-led one. Remember, you were never meant to run your business as the world does. But instead, be in full surrender to the Lord because He is the one Who has the strategy for you, but it starts with you giving it all to Him.

Next, we will talk about that weight on your shoulders that you should not be carrying.

CHAPTER 4

The Weight You Were Never Meant to Carry

When did business stop feeling like purpose?

There's a moment most of us can pinpoint when something that used to light us up now just wears us out.

You wake up feeling exhausted before your feet even hit the floor. You dread client calls. You question your pricing, your niche, and your entire existence as a business owner. Maybe you even wonder if you misheard God when you started this whole thing.

I've been there. We all have.

That moment when your business starts to feel heavy isn't always about the business itself; it's about the pressure you're carrying that God never told you to pick up.

And sis, let's be honest. Some of us are walking around with CEO titles and savior complexes. Trying to hold everything together, help everybody, meet every need, answer every message, and stay "humble" while doing it.

But can I tell you something in love?

You weren't built to be the provider. That's God's job.

You weren't designed to run on pressure. You were created to run on purpose.

The Warning Signs of Misalignment

Let's talk about the red flags.

You might be out of alignment if...

1. You're doing too much... but nothing feels fruitful.

You've got a full calendar but an empty tank. You're saying 'yes' to everything and secretly resenting it. That's not Kingdom stewardship; that's burnout wrapped in a bow of productivity.

2. You're making money... but losing peace.

You hit your income goal, but it doesn't feel like a win. You're stressed, snapping at your kids, skipping meals, and sleeping with your phone under your pillow. That's not abundance. That's survival in stilettos.

3. You feel guilty for wanting more... but frustrated with what you've built.

You love your business, but it's starting to feel like a cage instead of a calling. You crave time freedom, better clients, or a new direction, but you're afraid that pivoting means failure.

These are not signs of failure. They're invitations to realignment.

Pressure is Not a Prerequisite

We live in a culture that glorifies grinding, especially for women. Hustle is often worn like a badge of honor. If you're tired, overbooked, and undernourished, you must be doing it right.

But in the Kingdom, rest is a strategy.

Psalm 55:22 says, "Cast your cares on the Lord and he will sustain you; he will never let the righteous be shaken."

You don't need to earn God's provision through burnout. You don't need to prove your worth through overwork. What you do need is permission to lay it down and pick up grace instead.

So let me give you that permission:

You are allowed to say, ***"This isn't working anymore."***

You are allowed to build something different.

You are allowed to trade pressure for purpose.

Releasing What God Didn't Ask You to Carry

When business becomes heavy, it's usually because we're carrying things that weren't ours to begin with:

- Expectations other people placed on us
- Programs we launched out of panic, not purpose
- Clients we accepted because we needed the money
- Pricing we copied instead of prayed over

Let this be your moment of release. Write it down if you have to. Here's a simple prayer I've whispered more times than I can count:

"Lord, if You didn't tell me to build this, I don't want it. And if you did tell me to build it, show me how to do it without losing myself in the process."

Because here's the thing: God doesn't bless the version of your business that's built on fear. He blesses the one that's built on obedience.

Building With God, Not Just For Him

Many of us started our business for God... but somewhere along the line, we forgot to build it with Him.

There's a difference between:

Asking God to bless your plan;

And asking God to give you His plan.

The first one leads to burnout.

The second one leads to breakthroughs.

And friend, I know you want a breakthrough.

Not just financially but emotionally, spiritually, and in how you experience your business every day.

So if you're tired of dragging your business like a cross you were never meant to carry, this is your cue to set it down.

Let God show you how to build with Him again.

Reflection Questions (Let's Go Deeper)

Ready to realign? Here's a reset you can do today.

1. Ask: What am I carrying that feels heavy?

Make a list. Get honest. Is it a product that drains you? A schedule that exhausts you? A client that triggers anxiety?

2. Surrender: What needs to be released or restructured?

Take that list to God. Don't overthink it. Just pray: "Lord, help me see what's misaligned and give me the boldness to change it."

3. Rebuild: What does peace feel like in this season?

Design your next quarter around that. Peace is not the absence of problems. It's the presence of God in your process.

Psalm 127:1 says, "Unless the Lord builds the house, the builders labor in vain." Don't be afraid to start again with Him.

Chapter Summary

Business can get heavy when we carry what God never asked us to. But He offers us a lighter yoke and a holy blueprint.

Misalignment shows up as exhaustion, resentment, or discontent.

Pressure is not proof of purpose.

Rest is a strategy, not a reward.

Building with God leads to sustainability.

Surrender is your starting point, not your last resort.

This chapter is your permission slip to stop forcing what no longer fits. To rest in what God is doing. To build again with peace and purpose at the center.

Because this is the part where the burden lifts.

And the breakthrough begins.

In Chapter 5, we will talk about the importance of rest as a business owner.

Rest Is Not a Reward; It's a Revelation

Why are we so afraid to rest?

Let me ask you something. When was the last time you truly rested? Not a vacation with your laptop "just in case." Not Sunday afternoon folding laundry. I mean rest like soul-deep, phone-off, guilt-free, be still and know that He is God kind of rest.

Most women I mentor get quiet when I ask that.

Because somewhere along the way, we started treating rest like a reward you earn after you've hustled hard enough.

Like it's a luxury for the privileged, not a command from the Creator.

But rest isn't a suggestion; it's holy.

God created the world in six days and rested on the seventh. Not because he was tired. But because he was setting a rhythm.

If the Creator of the universe modeled rest, what makes us think we can skip it and still be whole?

The Lie of Constant Productivity

Let's call it out: We have been discipled by hustle more than by holiness.

Our culture says:

"Sleep when you're dead."

"You can rest after you hit your next goal."

"If you're not working, you're falling behind."

But the Kingdom says:

"Come to Me, all who are weary, and I will give you rest." *(Matthew 11:28)*

"In repentance and rest is your salvation." (Isaiah 30:15)

"Be still, and know that I am God." (Psalm 46:10)

That last one wrecks me every time. Be still… and know.

Sometimes we don't know because we won't be still long enough to hear.

When Business Becomes a Burden, Rest Becomes Resistance

The enemy loves to twist good things like business and turn them into burdens. And one of his favorite strategies is to convince us that resting means we're lazy, weak, or falling behind.

But rest is resistance. It's a way of saying:

"I trust God more than I trust my to-do list."

"I don't need to prove anything by working 24/7."

"I am not my results; I am God's daughter."

That's power, friend.

And in this culture of constant output, choosing to rest is one of the most radical faith moves you can make.

The Cost of Unrest

Let's talk about what happens when you don't rest:

You start resenting your business.

Your creativity dries up.

Your body crashes.

Your relationships suffer.

You become reactive instead of responsive.

And maybe the most dangerous of all? You stop hearing God clearly. Because noise and motion often drown out revelation.

Burnout doesn't always start with big dramatic moments. Sometimes it creeps in quietly one late night, one skipped devotional, one more "yes" when you knew God said "no."

You were never meant to run on fumes. You were meant to run with the Holy Spirit.

Reset the Rhythm

You don't need a sabbatical in the mountains to find rest. (Though if you have that option, take it!) Rest is about rhythm, not just retreat.

Here's how you can build it into your life and business:

1. Sabbath Strategy

Pick one day each week where you don't work. No content batching, no inbox checking, no quiet guilttrips. Just be. Worship. Play. Nap. Laugh. Reconnect with God and yourself.

2. Margin in Your Calendar

Leave a buffer between meetings. Schedule rest like you schedule calls. Seriously write "REST" on your calendar and don't cancel on yourself.

3. Rest Rituals Daily

Start your day with prayer before the phone. Stretch. Go for a walk. Breathe. Little rhythms add up.

4. Stop Glorifying the Grind

Rest is productive. Say that out loud. Write it on a sticky note if you have to. Rest is productive.

Jesus Rested Too

Let's not forget Jesus regularly withdrew to quiet places. He napped in boats. He escaped the crowd. He got alone with the Father.

If the Son of God needed time to refuel and reconnect, you do too.

This isn't about laziness. It's about longevity.

Burnout isn't just bad for business. It's bad for your calling.

Rest is Where Revelation Finds You

Do you know where some of your clearest directions will come from? Not a conference. Not a marketing coach. Not a 12-hour content creation binge.

But in the stillness. There have been times when I literally didn't know what else to do. I felt burned out. When I reach this roadblock, I always fall back on the Lord's word: ***"Be Still and Know I am God."***

When you're not trying to force clarity, you'll receive it.

Some of my best business ideas didn't come from whiteboards or strategy sessions.

They came in prayer. In rest. In worship. In the shower. In the car with no music on.

Because that's where I'm quiet enough to hear.

God is still speaking. He just needs you to slow down long enough to listen.

Reflection Questions (Let's Go Deeper)

1. When was the last time you rested on purpose, not because you were forced to?

Describe that moment. What did it feel like in your body, mind, and spirit? If you can't remember, what would it take to carve out a pocket of rest this week?

2. What lie about rest have you believed without realizing it?

Maybe it's "rest is for lazy people" or "if I stop, everything will fall apart." Write it down. Then speak truth over it. What does God actually say about rest?

3. Have you been treating rest as a reward for productivity instead of a rhythm of obedience?

How would your schedule shift if you planned rest like it mattered as much as work?

4. In what area of your life is hustle louder than the Holy Spirit?

Name the place where burnout is brewing. Then ask: What would resistance look like there? What could you say "no" to this week to protect your peace?

5. Try a 24-Hour Rest Reset

No work. No inbox. No checking to-do lists. Journal how your body and spirit feel before and after. Were there moments when clarity or conviction met you in the quiet?

Chapter Summary

Rest isn't weakness. It's wisdom.

You don't need to hustle harder. You need to trust deeper.

Rest is a rhythm, not a reward.

Burnout is a sign of disconnection. Jesus modeled rest, and so should we.

Margin is spiritual. Stillness brings clarity.

You weren't created to build your business at the expense of your soul.

So today, trade your striving for stillness. Trade your pressure for peace.

Rest is not what you do when you're done. It's what you need to keep going.

And in that holy pause, God will remind you who you are and Who's really in charge.

Have there been moments when nothing seems to be moving? It is like no matter what you do, you're just not going anywhere.

In Chapter 6, we will talk about when God hits pause on your progress.

When God Hits Pause on Your Progress

Sometimes the "No" is the setup for the "Next."

You thought this year would be the one. You finally invested in the coach, launched the new product, and prayed over the content calendar, and then nothing. Not a single sale. Not a single open door. Just crickets.

Ever been there?

That awkward in-between season where it feels like everyone else is soaring and you're still circling the runway, waiting for clearance to take off. You refresh your email. You rebuke your email. You wonder if you missed God completely.

I know that space.

But here's the truth most entrepreneurs don't want to admit out loud: Sometimes, God will hit pause on your progress for your protection, not your punishment.

The Illusion of Forward Motion

We live in a world obsessed with growth numbers, visibility, momentum, and success stories. It's easy to believe that if we're not constantly building, producing, or posting, we're falling behind.

But God doesn't move on our timeline or fit into our launch plans. He doesn't grade our obedience by how fast we scale.

In fact, some of the most powerful moves of God happen in the quiet. In the pause. In the space between vision and manifestation.

Just ask Joseph. Or Moses. Or you, right now.

The Pause is the Preparation

Think back to the children of Israel. God didn't send them straight from Egypt into the Promised Land. There was a wilderness first. And while the wilderness gets a bad rep, it was also a classroom.

In that pause:

God fed them.

He showed them His character.

He prepared them to steward the promise.

You see, what feels like a delay may actually be divine development.

"Be still, and know that I am God." - Psalm 46:10

Stillness doesn't mean stuck. Stillness is trust in action.

Why the Pause Feels So Painful

Let's be honest. The pause hurts more when:

You see others getting what you prayed for.

You know you've been faithful and obedient.

You're running out of financial margin and emotional energy.

But here's a gentle reminder: Comparison is a trap, and it will convince you that your pause is punishment while someone else's progress is proof.

But God's timeline is not your neighbor's timeline. He's not running late. He's working deeply.

"To everything there is a season, a time for every purpose under heaven." - Ecclesiastes 3:1

Even the pauses have purpose.

What to Do in the Pause

Let's talk about what you can do when it feels like the business is stuck:

1. Audit, Don't Abandon

Use the stillness to reflect, not retreat.

Look at what's working, what isn't, and where you're operating outside your grace lane.

Ask yourself:

Have I been doing too much in my own strength?

Is there an area where I've been disobedient?

Did I follow His instructions or just apply another strategy I saw online?

2. Rest Without Guilt

Resting doesn't mean you're lazy. Rest is holy. Even God rested.

Give yourself permission to:

Stop overthinking.

Take a break from creating.

Realign your heart before your strategy.

"In returning and rest you shall be saved; in quietness and confidence shall be your strength." - Isaiah 30:15

3. Refocus Your Why

Maybe you started your business to help people but got distracted chasing results.

The pause is the perfect time to return to your original why and submit it to God again.

Ask:

Who did I start this for?

Have I made this more about my validation than my vocation?

4. Prepare for the Release

Here's the thing: Every pause ends. Eventually, God releases you to move forward but how you wait matters.

Prepare like the breakthrough is already in motion. Because it is.

Update the offer. Finish the workbook. Record the video. Get your systems ready.

Even if nobody sees it yet... you're in training for your next season.

The Business May Be on Pause, But You're Not Forgotten

One of the biggest lies the enemy whispers during these seasons is, "God's done using you." He'll try to convince you that if it hasn't worked by now, it never will.

But let me tell you what I've learned from experience:

God often presses pause to clear out the noise, prune what isn't producing fruit, and sharpen your ability to hear Him clearly.

That's not a curse. That's love.

Kingdom Principle: Waiting is Working

When you wait well, you position yourself for overflow.

Isaiah 40:31 says:

"But those who wait on the Lord shall renew their strength. They shall mount up with wings like eagles..."

Notice it doesn't say those who hustle hardest. It says *those who wait.*

Not passive, defeated waiting. But intentional, hopeful, expectant waiting.

Reflection Questions (Let's Go Deeper)

1. Where in your business have you felt God hit "pause" recently?
2. What emotions come up when things slow down? Guilt, fear, anxiety?
3. What's one belief about success that needs to be surrendered?
4. How can you shift your mindset from pressure to preparation?

Chapter Summary

If your business feels stuck, it doesn't mean you're doing something wrong. It may mean God is doing something deeper. He's not ignoring you; He's growing you.

Pause is not punishment. Stillness is not failure.

Sometimes, the most strategic thing you can do for your business is be still and know.

Are you carrying weight that was not yours in the first place? Let's talk about that in Chapter 7.

The Weight That Was Never Yours

There's a difference between building with God and building for God. One will fuel you, the other will wear you out. I learned that the hard way.

There was a season in my business when I would stay up at night, staring at the ceiling, mentally counting invoices, bills, and prayer requests. And not one of them was paid with worry. Not one.

I was trying to carry what wasn't mine to carry.

Here's what I had to realize: Purpose carries power. Pressure depletes it.

God didn't call me to run a business so I could become the most tired, overworked version of myself. He called me to multiply what He gave me not to burn out trying to manufacture something He never assigned.

Let's take a look at a few common burdens Christian women entrepreneurs carry when they're not building in alignment with God's pace:

The Burden of Proving

You start off just wanting to help. Then somewhere along the way, you start hustling not for clients, but for validation.

You say 'yes' to projects that drain you.

You discount prices out of fear someone will say you're "too expensive."

You try to outperform everyone online, hoping to silence the voice that whispers, "You're not good enough."

But here's the truth: You don't need to prove anything God has already approved.

Romans 8:30 says, "Those He called, He also justified."

That means when God gave you that idea, He already factored in your learning curve, your gaps, your late nights, and your healing journey.

And he still said go.

The Burden of Perfection

Whew. This one used to have me in a chokehold.

I thought I had to wait until I had the perfect funnel, the perfect website, the perfect voice before I launched anything.

But in Matthew 14, Peter didn't wait until he mastered walking on water. He just stepped out.

Building with God is messy obedience. There's no version of Kingdom entrepreneurship that doesn't require some trial-and-error with a whole lot of grace.

Perfectionism is just fear in a sparkly outfit.

The Burden of Pace

Just because someone else hit six figures in six months doesn't mean that's your story.

Psalm 37:23 reminds us, "The steps of a good man are ordered by the Lord."

Not rushed. Ordered.

You are not behind.

You are not slow.

You're building with intention.

You're building for legacy.

And you're letting God set the tempo.

Because here's what no one tells you: When you rush, you recreate Egypt.

When you rest, you build Canaan.

What Alignment Actually Feels Like

So what does building in alignment feel like?

There's peace even when there's pressure.

There's clarity on what's for you and what's not.

There's fruit that feels like overflow, not overwork.

You'll still have deadlines. You'll still need a strategy. But you won't be trying to force something into existence without God's breath on it.

One morning, I lay awake in my bed, frustrated. My numbers weren't where I wanted them to be. I was second-guessing my offer, my audience, even my voice.

And the Lord whispered, "Did I tell you to stop?" I was so busy checking metrics, I forgot to check in with the Master. And that's when I remembered:

Your greatest metric is obedience.

Not followers.

Not revenue.

No email opens.

Obedience.

Reflection Questions (Let's Go Deeper)

If you're feeling pressure, ask yourself this:

"Am I trying to carry a result that only God can produce?"

Because purpose doesn't pressure you into burnout. It anchors you in obedience.

Chapter Summary

When business gets heavy, it's time to check alignment, not hustle harder.

Validation, perfection, and speed are common burdens but not yours to carry.

Peace and pressure can coexist when you're led by purpose.

Obedience is the new success metric.

Matthew 11:30 says, "My yoke is easy and My burden is light."

If it's heavy, you might be dragging something God never asked you to pick up.

Next, we will talk about being called but tired.

CHAPTER 8

When You're Called but Tired
(Ministry in the Mundane)

Some days, you don't feel powerful. You don't feel anointed. You don't feel anything but tired. And it's not the kind of tiredness a nap can fix.

You love God.

You love your calling.

But business feels like an uphill climb in muddy boots.

And if you've ever whispered to yourself, "God, I'm trying... but I'm tired," this chapter is for you.

Because here's what the enemy loves to do: use fatigue to blur your vision. Use busyness to bury your purpose. And make you believe that exhaustion is your new normal.

But God never called you to burnout. He called you to build.

You Can Be Called and Still Get Weary

Let's normalize this right now:

You can be called and still be tired.

You can be anointed and still feel overwhelmed.

You can love what you do and still feel burdened by it.

In fact, some of the greatest leaders in Scripture reached moments of breaking:

Elijah called down fire from heaven, then hid in a cave, asking God to take his life (**1 Kings 19:4**).

Moses led the people through the wilderness but got so frustrated that he hit the rock.

Jesus even said, ***"My soul is overwhelmed to the point of death" in Gethsemane (Matthew 26:38).***

You are in good company, sis.

Signs You're Carrying Your Business Instead of Letting God Build It

Here are some red flags that you've slipped into striving mode:

- You dread your inbox more than you enjoy serving your clients.
- Every decision feels like life or death.
- You haven't prayed about your business in weeks because you're afraid of what God might say.
- You keep saying "yes" to clients you're not called to just to avoid conflict or loss.

Here's the truth: God isn't glorified by your grind. He's glorified by your surrender.

Psalm 127:1 says, "Unless the Lord builds the house, those who build it labor in vain."

You're not just a CEO; you're a co-laborer with Christ.

Rest is a Weapon, Not a Reward

Rest isn't what you do when you've earned it.

Rest is what you do when you trust God to run things without your hands all over it.

Let me say that again: Rest is faith in action.

When you pause, when you unplug, when you say 'no' out of obedience instead of fear, you are declaring, **"God, I trust You to sustain this."**

That's powerful. That's Kingdom. That's alignment.

In Genesis 2:2, God rested. Not because he was tired, but because he was finished.

Your rest doesn't signal weakness. It signals completion.

What to Do When You Feel Stuck

If your business feels stuck or stale, here are three things to pray through:

1. *Realign*: Ask God, "Did I step into something I wasn't assigned to?"

Sometimes the burnout is tied to busywork God never approved.

2. *Release*: Are there clients, offers, or expectations you need to let go of?

Just because it worked last year doesn't mean it fits this season.

3. *Recommit*: Get quiet. Go back to your journal. Look at what God told you before the overwhelm hit. You may not need a new strategy. You may need renewed surrender.

Your Business Is a Garden, Not a Machine

Machines need constant input to function. They break down when overused.

Gardens, on the other hand, require rhythms: seed time and harvest. Sun and rain. Waiting and working.

Stop treating your business like a machine. Start treating it like a garden.

Sow with intention.

Water with prayer.

Pull up the weeds of comparison.

Celebrate the small sprouts.

Zechariah 4:10 reminds us, "Do not despise these small beginnings, for the Lord rejoices to see the work begin."

Reflection Questions (Let's Go Deeper)

1. What is one area of your business where tiredness has turned into avoidance?

Have you been putting something off not because it's hard, but because you're worn out? Get honest with yourself about what's been draining you more than it's been growing you.

2. Are you carrying more than what God asked you to carry?

List out everything you are managing right now in your business. Circle the ones you never asked God about. Ask Him which assignments were meant for *this* season and which ones need to be surrendered.

3. When was the last time you felt true joy in your business?

Write about a moment where you felt aligned, excited, or even just peacefully on track. What was different then? What can you bring back into your daily rhythm?

4. What does rest look like in this season, not just in theory but practically?

Identify one way you can build rest into your current week. Not vacation. Not a three-day retreat. Just one, small, intentional act of holy stillness. Then write how you'll protect it.

5. If your business was a garden, what part of it needs weeding, watering, or waiting?

Use the garden metaphor: What are you trying to force to bloom? Where are you overwatering with effort instead of trusting God to bring increase? What needs pruning?

Chapter Summary

You can be tired and still be called. But you don't have to stay in the struggle.

Your weariness is not a sin; it's a signal.

God builds differently than the world.

Rest isn't quitting; it's trusting.

You are allowed to grow slowly.

You don't have to build in burnout mode.

"Come to Me, all who are weary and burdened, and I will give you rest." - Matthew 11:28

Sometimes obedience feels risky, but what do we do when that is the case? We will discuss this in Chapter 9.

When Obedience Feels Risky
(That Gut-Wrenching Yes)

Have you ever said "yes" to God... and immediately wanted to take it back?

Maybe you left a job that felt safe.

Or launched an offer that made zero sense on paper.

Or forgave someone who never apologized.

Obedience sounds holy. And it is.

But it can also feel like stepping into the fog with no flashlight, no backup plan, and a whole lot of "Lord, are You sure?"

This chapter is for the woman who said 'yes'... and then watched her comfort zone catch fire.

When the Step of Faith Costs More Than You Expected

These six steps will guide you through the process of allowing God to help you move in the direction He has for you without feeling overwhelmed.

1. Obedience is not always logical.

When I felt God prompting me to shift my business model, I thought, "Okay, Lord. Let's do this."

Then came the silence. The slow months. The empty calendar.

I remember thinking, "I thought this was your idea."

But God doesn't always show fruit before faith. Sometimes He's testing:

Will you follow me even if it gets uncomfortable?

Like Abraham leaving everything to walk into the unknown (**Genesis 12**). He wasn't given a map, just a promise.

Faith doesn't ask for proof. It walks with purpose.

2. Obedience vs. Outcome: Why You're Not Responsible for Results

One of the biggest lies the enemy whispers is: "If this was really from God, it would've worked by now."

But Kingdom math doesn't follow earthly timelines.

Your obedience is the win even if you don't see the harvest immediately.

Remember Noah? That man built a boat when it had never rained. Do you know how long people must have mocked him?

Sometimes obedience looks like wasting time to everyone else but it's worship to God.

Isaiah 55:8 reminds us, "My thoughts are not your thoughts, neither are your ways my ways."

You don't carry the outcome. You just carry the assignment.

3. Signs You're Obeying God, Not Hustle Culture

Here's how to tell the difference between Holy Spirit direction and hustle-driven decisions:

Let's be honest. It's easy to say "God is CEO" on Instagram. It's harder to let Him call the shots behind the scenes.

But obedience builds a legacy. Hustle builds a reputation.

Only one stands when storms come.

4. Obedience Often Looks Like Loss at First

Yes, it might cost you.

Relationships that don't get your Kingdom vision.

Clients who loved the old version of you.

Money you thought would come faster.

But what you lose in comfort, you gain in clarity.

When I let go of doing what "worked" in the world's eyes and leaned into what God was asking, I found peace. Not instant profit. Not instant applause. But peace.

And that peace is what sustained me while the harvest grew underground.

Luke 9:24 says, "Whoever wants to save their life will lose it, but whoever loses their life for Me will save it."

This applies to business, too, lovely. Let it go if He said so.

5. What Radical Obedience Looks Like in Business

Radical obedience might sound dramatic, but it's often small and consistent.

Pricing your services in alignment with your worth, even if someone walks away.

Choosing integrity when shortcuts look easier.

Saying no to opportunities that pull you out of your lane.

Resisting the urge to "rebrand" every 30 days out of fear you're not enough.

It's trusting that God will send your clients, not just your marketing strategy.

Obedience is the new strategy. Faith is the new funnel.

Reflection Questions (Let's Go Deeper)

1. What has obedience recently cost you and was it worth it?

Write down a time you said "yes" to God in business, even when it didn't make sense. Did it feel like a loss at first? What fruit came from it that you might have missed if you waited for it to be convenient?

2. Where have you confused results with responsibility?

Be honest. Are you trying to force an outcome God never asked you to carry? What would it feel like to lay that outcome back at His feet and simply stay faithful to the assignment?

3. Are you building your business from obedience or old habits?

Look at the systems, offers, or decisions you've made recently. Which ones came from peace and prayer and which came from pressure and "what worked before?" What needs to shift?

4. Have you been scared to say 'yes' again because of how the last one felt?

That last "yes" might have been painful or lonely. Are you letting that disappointment keep you from obeying again? Ask God what healing you need before moving forward in faith.

5. What does radical obedience look like for you today, not next month, not next year?

Is it a conversation you've been avoiding? A pivot you've been delaying? A "yes" you've been scared to say out loud? Write it down. Then pray for the courage to walk into the fog anyway, knowing God walks with you.

Chapter Summary

Let's bring it home.

Obedience isn't just for church pews. It's for boardrooms, launch plans, contracts, and pricing.

Obedience may cost dis-comfort, but it is the birth's purpose. You're not responsible for results, just your yes.

Hustle looks busy.

Obedience looks surrendered.

Loss is often part of the process, but peace is the promise.

Radical faith in business may not trend but it will transform.

"Trust in the Lord with all your heart, and lean not on your own understanding." - Proverbs 3:5

God's way isn't always the fastest. But it's always the most fruitful.

Next, in Chapter 10, we will explore how we can find grace in the grind.

Finding Grace in the Grind
(Why Does This Feel So Hard?)

You're doing what God told you to do.

You've obeyed. You've prayed. You've planned.

But still... It feels heavy.

Not hard because you're lazy.

Not heavy because you're doing it wrong.

But just... heavy.

This chapter is about those moments. The ones where it feels like everyone else has a team, a cushion, and 30 hours in their day, while you're running on fumes and faith. Let's talk about what grace really looks like when you're in the trenches of building something God ordained, but emotionally and spiritually exhausting.

Grace Isn't a Shortcut; It's a Strength

Somewhere along the way, we confused grace with ease.

But grace isn't a pass that keeps you from struggling; it's the fuel that helps you keep going when everything in you wants to quit.

Paul understood this.

He pleaded three times for the thorn in his flesh to be taken away (2 Corinthians 12). But what did God say? "My grace is sufficient for you, for my power is made perfect in weakness."

We want God to remove the thorn.

He wants to strengthen us in spite of it.

That grace shows up in the late nights, the client disappointments, the launch flops, and the unpaid invoices. And it whispers, "Keep going. I'm with you."

The Trap of Comparing Your Calling

Nothing makes your business feel heavier than watching someone else's success.

You're scrolling on Instagram.

You see another coach celebrating a five-figure launch.

Another business owner got booked for a podcast.

Someone else went viral for doing the exact thing you just did last week with crickets.

Comparison robs you of clarity. And clarity is where purpose lives.

Let's be real: You don't know what grace they need for their assignment.

Your calling is not copy-paste. It's custom-built.

When God designed you, He didn't borrow someone else's blueprint.

Psalm 139:14 says you're "fearfully and wonderfully made."

That includes your business model, your pace, your clients, and your capacity.

Stay in your lane. Grace runs strongest there.

When the Grind Becomes a God

We don't say it out loud, but hustle can become an idol.

We start thinking productivity equals purpose.

We believe the more we do, the more faithful we are.

But God never called you to be His assistant.

He's not impressed by your 90-hour workweek.

He's not moved by burnout in His name.

He's after your obedience, not your overexertion.

Remember Martha and Mary? *(Luke 10:38-42)*

Martha was busy doing the "good stuff," serving Jesus.

Mary was sitting at His feet.

Guess who Jesus praised?

He said, "Only one thing is necessary. Mary has chosen what is better."

Sometimes the holiest thing you can do is sit down.

Building with God Requires Rhythms, Not Rushing

We like to sprint. God prefers a steady walk.

Look at how He built the world day by day, with margin.

Even Jesus rested. The Savior of the world took naps *(Mark 4:38)*. So why are we allergic to rest?

Here's what I've learned:

If you don't create rhythms of grace, your body will create crashes for you.

Sabbaths are not optional.

Prayer isn't a side dish; it's the strategy.

Delegating isn't a weakness; it's wisdom.

Business isn't about how fast you can build; it's about how faithfully you can sustain.

What Grace in Business Actually Looks Like

Let's make this super practical.

Grace in business might look like:

Saying 'no' to an opportunity that doesn't align, even if it's lucrative.

Taking a nap instead of pushing through another 12-hour day.

Charging your worth without guilt.

Pausing a launch because your spirit says, "Not right now."

Firing a client who drains your peace.

Grace is a boundary.

Grace is a pace.

Grace is a permission slip to stop performing.

Business gets heavy when you carry things God never told you to pick up.

Reflection Questions (Let's Go Deeper)

1. What thorn are you asking God to move from you?

Write down those things in your business and personal life that you want God to move from you.

2. How are you comparing yourself to other people?

Be honest. Is this comparison giving you anxiety? What would it feel like if, instead of comparing your business or yourself to others, you surround yourself and your business with the Lord?

3. Have you allowed the busyness to become an idol?

Look at the times when you are consumed by everything you have to do. In what ways has productivity quietly replaced presence in your walk with God and in your business decisions?

4. What rhythms of grace are missing from your week right now?

Think about your week, what would it look like to rebuild your schedule around rest instead of rush?

5. Is there something you picked up out of fear, pressure, or obligation that God never actually asked you to carry, and are willing to put down?

How would your business and personal life change if you allowed God to do all the heavy lifting? Would you have more peace, more motivation, and better clarity?

Chapter Summary

If business feels like a boulder, ask yourself: Am I building this with God or just for God? Grace isn't ease; it's empowerment.

Comparison clutters your clarity.

Hustle can become a false god.

Rhythms protect your peace.

Obedience includes rest, boundaries, and Spirit-led pivots.

"Come to Me, all who are weary and burdened, and I will give you rest." - Matthew 11:28

You don't have to grind for what God already gave.

What if I told you that surrender isn't quitting but a strategy, let's talk about that next in Chapter 11.

Surrender Isn't Quitting; It's Strategy
(The Lie We Tell Ourselves)

How many times have you whispered, "I just need to push through?"

Push through the exhaustion.

Push through the confusion.

Push through the financial drought, the spiritual fog, and the lack of clarity.

We wear "grind mode" like a badge of honor, but behind it is often fear.

Here's the truth most of us don't want to say out loud:

We're scared that surrender looks like failure.

That if we slow down, everything will fall apart.

That if we don't hold it all together, no one will.

But here's the Kingdom twist:

Surrender is not quitting.

It's letting God be CEO.

The Myth of Control

We say we trust God... but we keep our fingers clenched around the outcome.

I remember launching a program once, convinced it was "the one." I had the graphics, the emails, and the strategy. But no clients. Just crickets and confusion.

I wanted to fix it. Rework it. Hustle harder.

But God said, "Hand it over."

Not tweak. Not fixed. Surrender.

That moment was humbling but holy. Because control is a heavy burden. And it's not yours to carry.

Proverbs 16:9 says, "We can make our plans, but the Lord determines our steps."

When you release control, you make room for divine strategy.

What Surrender Really Looks Like

Let's be real, surrender isn't passive. It's not lying on the couch, hoping clients fall from the sky.

Surrender is active trust.

It looks like:

Praying before planning.

Saying no to shiny distractions that don't align with your calling.

Tithing faithfully even when money feels tight.

Walking away from what looks "successful" but feels spiritually heavy.

Creating space to hear what God wants you to build, not just what your niche says is trending.

It's not about doing nothing.

It's about doing the right things with the right heart posture.

When God Redirects Your Blueprint

Some of the most Spirit-filled businesses didn't begin with clarity. They began with chaos and obedience.

Moses didn't feel ready.

Esther didn't ask to be queen.

Ruth didn't plan to move to Bethlehem, broke and widowed.

But each one made a faith move, and God met them in it.

So if your blueprint is unraveling, don't panic.

That might be God tearing up the version you wrote… to give you one that aligns with His vision.

Isaiah 55:89 reminds us, "My thoughts are not your thoughts, neither are your ways my ways."

And thank goodness for that, because His way is always better.

The Blessing Hidden in Letting Go

Letting go might look like:

Closing a program that's profitable but draining your peace.

Pausing a launch because you need spiritual clarity, not another funnel.

Saying 'no' to a client who doesn't align with your values.

Creating boundaries around your time, even if it costs you income upfront.

The world will say, "You're crazy for walking away."

But your spirit will whisper, "That was obedience."

When you surrender, you activate the blessing of release.

And make no mistake, obedience might look foolish to others, but it positions you for overflow.

Practicing Surrender in Your Daily Business Life

Here are some practical ways to cultivate a surrendered business rhythm:

Morning check-ins with God. Before emails, messages, or to-do lists, ask: "Lord, what's the assignment today?"

Build margin in your calendar. Overbooked calendars create undernourished spirits.

Track obedience over outcomes. What did God tell you to do, and did you do it? That's your KPI.

Schedule the actual Sabbath. Not just "Netflix and rest" but intentional space to delight in God.

Your business doesn't just need more strategy. It needs more surrender.

Reflection Questions (Let's Go Deeper)

1. Where in your business or life do you feel like God hit pause or pulled you off course?
2. How do you normally respond when things don't go "according to plan"? Is it faith... or frustration?
3. What would it look like to trust that *this* redirection is divine protection?
4. Are you forcing anything right now that God might be trying to *free* you from?
5. What's one thing you can release this week to make space for realignment?

Chapter Summary

Sometimes God *slams* the door you were begging Him to open. Not because he's cruel. Because you're aiming too low. This chapter hits the heart of what we all face in leadership: the tension between obedience and control. You set the plan. You did the work. And then boom, silence, setbacks, or a sharp pivot you didn't ask for. But here's the truth: Realignment is not rejection. It's God's way of saying, "I've got something better... if you'll stop forcing this."

Maybe it's time to walk through how to *sit with the stillness*, drop the striving, and let God *reposition* you instead of you spiraling. Because control is exhausting. And trust? That's where the peace is.

In Chapter 12, we address using rest as your weapon...

What Rest Really Means When You're a Christian Entrepreneur
(When Rest Feels Like a Luxury You Can't Afford)

Let's be honest.

When you're the one who wears all the hats: CEO, marketing team, accountant, prayer warrior, and Uber driver for your kids, rest can feel like rebellion.

Because the world teaches us to build by pushing.

To scale by striving.

To prove our value by how much we can produce.

But rest is not a reward for burning out.

It's a command. A blessing. A trust move.

"Come to me, all you who are weary and burdened, and I will give you rest." - Matthew 11:28

Jesus didn't say, "I'll give you more strategy."

He said, "I will give you rest."

The Hustle Trap (And Why Even Good Hustle Is Still Heavy)

Hustle isn't just a schedule problem; it's a heart problem.

You can be busy building for God but still disconnected from Him.

And here's the wild thing: Hustle doesn't always look like sin.

It can look like a church service, posting faith-based content, running a Christian business...

But if it's rooted in fear, scarcity, or pressure to prove yourself, it's still bondage.

I used to think rest would come after I hit the next milestone.

The next client. The next launch. The next payment.

But God showed me that if I can't rest with a little, I won't rest with a lot.

Because striving doesn't leave when the money comes.

It leaves when your identity is no longer attached to what you produce.

What the Bible Really Says About Rest

Let's take it back to the beginning.

God created the world in six days. Then he rested.

Now think about that.

The Creator of the universe... the One who never grows weary... took a full day to rest.

Not because he needed a nap.

But because He was showing us a rhythm of life.

"Six days you shall labor and do all your work, but the seventh day is a sabbath to the Lord your God." - Exodus 20:9-10

This wasn't a suggestion. It was a command.

And not just for Sunday service either.

Sabbath is sacred.

It's a declaration that God is your Source, not your hustle.

The Cost of Skipping Rest

Let's call it out.

When we skip rest:

We make more mistakes.

We burn out.

We start resenting the business God gave us.

We lead from emptiness, not overflow.

Rest isn't a weakness.

It's a power move.

The enemy would love for you to stay too tired to be effective.

Because a burnt-out believer is easier to distract than a rested one on assignment.

So, if you're always "on," never off, and feeling spiritually foggy...

You might not need another strategy session.

You might need a nap and some silence with God.

Redefining Rest as Resistance

In this culture, rest is radical.

It's choosing to pause when the algorithm says, "Post more."

It's logging off when your competitors are doubling their content output.

It's saying, "No, thank you" to opportunities that would drain your margin.

It's taking a walk, not for steps but for stillness.

Rest is a weapon. It silences fear.

It says, "I trust God enough to stop."

And in a world that glorifies burnout, rest becomes resistance.

What Rest Looks Like in Real Life

Let's break it down in simple, everyday choices:

Soulcare over selfcare. Bubble baths are nice, but don't neglect worship, journaling, and being still in His presence.

One day off a week. No planning. No content. No work. Just rest, delight, and reconnect with your why.

Margin in your schedule. Stop booking every hour. Leave room for overflow and peace.

Boundaries that protect your calling. You don't have to say 'yes' to everything just because you can.

And let's be clear, rest doesn't mean you don't work hard.

It means you don't overwork from fear.

Reflection Questions (Let's Go Deeper)

1. Where have you equated your worth with your output?
2. What lie have you believed about rest that needs to die today?
3. How would your business shift if you built from overflow instead of burnout?
4. When was the last time you scheduled rest, not collapse?
5. What boundaries need to be put in place to protect your peace?

Chapter Summary

Let's kill the lie that rest is lazy. Because rest is *warfare*. In a world that idolizes hustle and runs on burnout, let us flip the script: Rest is not a reward for exhaustion, it's a *strategy for expansion*. The Sabbath isn't about slowing down; it's about *reclaiming* your rhythm and refusing to let busyness be your boss.

This chapter is a call-out and a call-in for every woman who's been grinding herself into the ground, thinking, *"If I just do more, I'll get ahead."* No. Rest is holy. Rest is obedience. Rest is how you *hear* again. You don't need more productivity hacks. You need permission to pause, and here it is.

Rest isn't a reward for your hustle. It's a rhythm that reflects your trust.

Rest is a Kingdom principle, not a productivity hack.

Hustle becomes toxic when it replaces intimacy with God.

You don't have to earn rest when you receive it.

Sabbath creates space for God to speak, refill, and realign you.

Rest is resistance in a world that glorifies burnout.

"In repentance and rest is your salvation, in quietness and trust is your strength." - Isaiah 30:15

Rest is not a luxury. It's a leadership decision.

So take a breath, sis.

The world will not fall apart if you pause because you weren't meant to hold it all together anyway.

In Chapter 13, we will talk about allowing yourself to pivot.

You're Allowed to Pivot
(When What You Built No Longer Fits)

Have you ever looked at your business and thought...

"This isn't what I signed up for."

Or maybe, "I used to love this, but now it feels heavy."

You're not crazy. You're just evolving.

God is maturing you. And sometimes that means what worked in one season is not right for this one.

There's no shame in pivoting.

What's shameful is staying stuck in something just because it's familiar.

In the Kingdom, obedience always outranks comfort.

The Myth of "Finish What You Started"

From childhood, we're taught to finish what we start.

But what happens when what you started was never supposed to last forever?

What if God only needed you to do that thing for a season?

That doesn't make it a failure.

That makes it an assignment completed.

Let's take it to Scripture:

"There is a time for everything, and a season for every activity under the heavens." - Ecclesiastes 3:1

Some of us are clinging to expired assignments because we're afraid of looking flaky, uncommitted, or like we made a mistake.

But guess what? Jesus pivoted.

His ministry shifted constantly. Sometimes, he preached to crowds. Sometimes, he withdraws.

Sometimes, He healed in public. Sometimes, he tells people, "Don't tell anyone."

The assignment didn't change. But the method did.

So if the Savior of the world pivoted... why can't you?

Signs It's Time to Pivot

Not every hard thing means it's time to quit. But here are some clues you might be due for a pivot:

Your peace is gone. You feel heavy, not just tired. There's no grace in it anymore.

You're operating from obligation. You dread the work you used to enjoy.

You feel boxed in. Your vision has expanded, but your brand, offer, or client no longer fits.

And here's a big one:

God has been whispering, but you've been avoiding the conversation.

He's not punishing you. He's inviting you to something new.

The Fear of Starting Over

Whew. This one hits hard.

The fear of pivoting is really the fear of starting from scratch... again.

"What will people think?"

"Will I lose everything I built?"

"Am I being irresponsible?"

But one thing I realized is that ...

When God calls you to pivot, you're not starting over; you're starting smarter. It was like my move to the US; I only knew the people I worked with. I had no family in the US, but God was with me...

In other words, starting over, you're not empty-handed.

You're carrying experience, wisdom, scars, and lessons.

Even Jesus had to leave Nazareth to step into his purpose.

Sometimes, the pivot is what positions you for the next level.

When the Brand Is Too Small for the Calling

Some businesses aren't broken; they're just too small for what God is building through you now.

That Etsy shop? It might've been the seed.

That coaching offer? It might've been the training ground.

But now, God's calling you to write, speak, launch, scale, or serve in a different way.

I can relate to this so well. I started writing with my first anthology, *InspireHer: Embracing Change and Transformation*, with my chapter *Rise Above: Turning Pain into Purpose*. This was the beginning of sharing my embarrassing story to bring healing to many women. Did I stop being a business coach? Of course not.

In other words, it doesn't mean you dishonor what you've built.

It means you submit it back to the One who gave it to you in the first place.

Let Him prune it, stretch it, rebrand it, or retire it.

He's not wasteful.

If He's shifting it, there's something greater on the other side.

Pivoting with Wisdom, Not Panic

There's a difference between pivoting because God said so and pivoting because you're discouraged.

Discouragement says: "This is too hard. I'm out."

Discernment says: "This season is shifting. It's time to move."

Here's how to pivot wisely:

- Pray and journal. Let God speak into your next step.
- Clarify your new vision. Don't pivot into confusion. Get clear.
- Map the bridge. How will you transition clients, messaging, or offers?
- Talk to your people. Let your audience grow with you. Authenticity builds trust.

And finally, give yourself permission to evolve. You don't need a tragedy or breakdown to justify a shift.

Sometimes, growth alone is enough reason to pivot.

Reflection Questions (Let's Go Deeper)

1. What part of your business (or life) feels misaligned but you've been too scared to change?
2. Are you clinging to something just because it worked in a past season?
3. If you stopped trying to "make it make sense," what would you be free to explore?

4. What have you been whispering to yourself that you're too afraid to say out loud?
5. Where is God inviting you to evolve, but you're still trying to explain?

Chapter Summary

Repeat after me: *You don't owe your past self a lifelong commitment to something God is asking you to leave.* This chapter is your permission slip to pivot without guilt, without explanation, and without dragging dead weight into your next season.

Let me dismantle the myth that "starting over" means failure. No, sis. Starting over is a strength. That nagging feeling you've outgrown what you built? It's not confusing. It's *confirmation*. When the grace lifts, you'd better follow. Because comfort isn't your calling, obedience is.

Pivoting is not failure. It's faith in motion. There is no shame in outgrowing an assignment.

Jesus pivoted. So can you.

Your pivot is not a restart; it's a rebuild with God's blueprint.

Peace is a signal. Don't ignore it.

Wisdom + obedience = a purpose-filled pivot

"Forget the former things; do not dwell on the past. See, I am doing a new thing!" - Isaiah 43:18-19

God is not finished with you.

He's just repositioning you for what's next.

Are you ready to follow Him even if it looks unfamiliar?

What do you do when God hits the reset button on your business?

Let's discuss it in Chapter 14.

When God Hits Reset on Your Business (It Was Working Until It Wasn't)

There's nothing quite like building something with your bare hands... only to watch God gently say, "We're going to do it differently now."

It's jarring.

Especially when everything was "fine" on the outside.

The bills were getting paid. Clients were coming. Your business had rhythm.

But inside? You knew it was off.

And then God does what only He can do. He shifts it all.

Sometimes gently. Sometimes, like a wrecking ball.

This chapter is for the woman who knows what it's like to have God hit reset on her business.

It's not punishment. It's preparation.

When God Disrupts What You Built

Let's go there.

You prayed for the business.

You dedicated it to Him.

You honored Him with your tithe.

You used Scripture in your content and prayed before client calls.

So when things started breaking down, it didn't make sense.

You asked:

"God... why would you let this fall apart?"

But what if it's not falling apart...

What if He's tearing down what was built in your strength so He can rebuild in His?

You might be grieving the loss of a business model, an audience, or an offer you thought was "the one."

But God isn't breaking you. He's rebuilding with you.

*"Unless the Lord builds the house, the builders labor in vain."
- Psalm 127:1*

He's Not Mad, He's Merciful

Let's settle this now.

The shift you're going through isn't because you messed up.

It's because He loves you too much to let you stay in a version of success that's misaligned.

God disciplines those He loves.

But He also redirects those He's about to bless.

He's not slamming doors out of anger. He's guarding your destiny.

That client ghosted? That launch flopped? That product that stopped selling?

It might not be sabotage, it might be a setup.

And sometimes the only way God can get your attention is to let things shake.

Reset Looks Like Obedience, Not Logic

When God resets your business, it rarely makes sense.

You might hear Him say:

"Take that offer down."

"Close the program."

"Cancel that launch."

"Rest for 90 days."

And everything in you will want to resist.

Because the world says, *Hustle*. But God says, *Heed my voice*.

Remember Noah? He built an ark with no rain in sight.

Remember Abraham? He packed up everything without knowing the destination.

God's version of alignment often looks like disruption first... and clarity later.

The Identity Crisis That Comes with Reset

Let's be honest, when God hits reset, it can feel like an identity crisis.

You ask:

"If I'm not that coach, then who am I?"

"If I'm not making money that way anymore, what do I tell people I do?"

"If I rest... will they forget me?"

This is where the real spiritual work begins.

God will strip away the titles, the likes, the offers, and the outcomes until all that's left is you and Him.

And that's where the real foundation gets laid.

You weren't called to build your image.

You were called to build the Kingdom.

Practical Ways to Walk Through a Reset Season

Reset seasons can be disorienting. Here's how to walk through them with faith and not fear:

- **Journal your prayers.**

  Write what you're hearing and feeling. Let God speak into your confusion.

- **Evaluate the fruit.**

  What feels forced? Where is the peace missing?

  Strip it back to the basics.

  What did God say originally? Go back to the blueprint.

- **Talk to trusted counsel.**

  Don't go through this alone. Find Spirit-filled business sisters or mentors to walk with you.

- **Wait before rebuilding.**

  This is key. Don't slap a new offer together just to soothe your ego.

Sit still long enough to let the right assignment emerge.

Reflection Questions (Let's Go Deeper)

1. What "gap" season are you currently navigating, and how are you labeling it: delay or development?

2. How has your frustration with not knowing "what's next" affected your obedience today?

3. Where do you feel God growing your faith, even if the results aren't visible yet?

4. What past gap did God use to develop something you now value?

5. What new meaning can you assign to the wait so it becomes worship instead of worry?

Chapter Summary

Let's talk about what happens between the promise and the payoff in that messy, stretching, uncomfortable *middle*. I call it: the *gap*. The part no one preaches about. Where nothing's working, doors aren't opening, and doubt moves in like an uninvited guest.

But what if the gap isn't punishment? What if it's where God grows your *capacity*?

This chapter exposes our addiction to clarity and shows why God gives *grace* instead. You'll never build what He called you to if you keep panicking in the in-between. This is where you stop fighting the fog and start trusting His footsteps.

God's reset isn't rejection. It's refined.

Just because something was God doesn't mean it still is.

Reset seasons are sacred even when they're scary.

You're not being punished. You're being positioned.

Identity must come from God, not what you produce.

Don't rush the rebuild. Let God lead the blueprint.

"Behold, I am doing a new thing… do you not perceive it?"
- Isaiah 43:19

God is not just rebuilding your business.

He's rebuilding you as a vessel of purpose, obedience, and Kingdom impact.

Even if it feels quiet now...

Even if no one claps for your pivot...

Even if it looks like you're starting from scratch...

Trust this: He is not done. He's just getting started in a whole new way.

The gap is not wasted time, it's a training ground. Let's talk now about the purpose in the pause as we move into Chapter 15.

The Purpose in the Pause
(When the Hustle Stops and Heaven Speaks)

There comes a moment in every faith-filled businesswoman's journey when she realizes she can't keep going at this pace.

Not just physically.

Spiritually.

Emotionally.

Mentally.

It's not burnout from laziness; it's exhaustion from carrying what God never asked her to carry alone.

This chapter is for the woman God put on pause.

Not as punishment.

But as protection.

This is the pause that pivots everything.

Slowing Down Isn't Quitting, It's Obedience

We often equate movement with progress.

"If I'm not launching…"

"If I'm not showing up online…"

"If I'm not constantly planning the next thing…"

Then clearly I'm not building.

But in God's economy, stillness is a strategy.

"Be still, and know that I am God." - Psalm 46:10

When you pause, you don't lose your momentum; you shift your reliance.

You stop drawing from your own power and begin leaning into God's presence.

The Holy Tension Between Rest and Responsibility

You've got bills.

You've got clients.

You've got a calling.

So when God says "Rest," it feels like a contradiction.

But He's not asking you to neglect what's in your hands.

He's asking you to let Him guide your grip.

Rest doesn't mean irresponsibility.

It means releasing the pressure to sustain yourself.

True rest is faith in motion.

What the Pause Reveals

Here's what no one tells you:

The pause will mess with your identity.

When your worth is tied to output, silence feels like failure.

But the pause reveals:

Where you were hustling in your own strength.

Where you built systems around fear.

Where your trust was more in Stripe than Scripture.

And friend... that revelation is a gift.

God doesn't reveal to shame you.

He reveals so He can rebuild you.

What to Do When God Says "Not Yet"

This is where most women squirm.

You got the download.

You made the plan.

You were ready to execute.

And then God whispered:

"Not yet."

This is the season where many jump ahead of God out of fear, only to land back in confusion.

But what if "not yet" is His "I love you" in disguise?

Here's how to wait well:

Stay in the Word. Let God's promises anchor you.

Tend to what's in front of you. Just because that new thing is paused doesn't mean everything is.

Process with God, not just your planner. Pause the productivity apps and pick up your prayer journal.

The Ministry of Margin

The pause is where margin is born.

When God pulls you back, He's making space for:

Healing you didn't know you needed.

Provision you couldn't have planned.

Vision you would've missed in hustle mode.

Margin isn't laziness.

It's a ministry.

It's where creativity breathes.

Where strategy downloads.

Where divine timing replaces forced timing.

God is not in a rush.

You don't have to be either.

Reflection Questions (Let's Go Deeper)

1. Where has busyness been your way of avoiding stillness with God?
2. What parts of your identity feel shaky when you're not producing?
3. What might God be healing, revealing, or realigning in this pause?
4. Are you waiting for permission to rest when God already gave it?
5. What would it look like to see margin not as a gap, but as grace?

Chapter Summary

Sometimes, God will *pause* your plans not to punish you but to protect you. This chapter is for the woman who's been running on empty and thinks that slowing down means losing momentum. But Andrea reminds us: Stillness isn't quitting. It's obedience.

When the hustle stops, Heaven speaks. That pause? It's where your grip loosens, your ears open, and your identity gets rebuilt. It reveals where you've been relying on your own strength, and calls you back to dependence on God. You thought the "not yet" meant denial, but it was divine protection. It's in the margin, not the grind, where miracles, clarity, and healing start to flow.

This isn't lost time. It's *launch prep*.

The most faith-filled thing you can do is pause on purpose.

Stillness isn't failure; it's spiritual warfare.

Pausing doesn't delay your purpose; it deepens it.

The wait will refine you if you let it.

Rest isn't a detour, it's a doorway to revelation.

"In returning and rest you shall be saved; in quietness and in trust shall be your strength." - Isaiah 30:15

This is the part of your journey where your roots grow deeper than your reach.

Let them.

God's building something in the pause that hustle never could.

Sometimes, obedience doesn't always feel like success. Believe me, I know it all too well.

In the next chapter, we will discuss what happens when you stay obedient to the Lord's word.

CHAPTER 16

What Happens When You Stay Obedient
(Obedience Does Not Always Feel Like Success)

Let's be honest, obedience can feel anticlimactic. You say 'yes' to God, and instead of fireworks and applause, you get crickets. You expect breakthroughs and instead get silence. And yet... something shifts inside. Peace shows up where striving used to live. Confidence walks in where confusion sits.

We like stories that end in neat bows, where obedience is followed by instant reward. But sometimes, obedience simply closes the chapter on stress and begins the quiet work of healing. That, my friend, is still a miracle. Even if nobody else claps for it.

Staying Doesn't Mean Stuck

A lot of people assume that staying where God placed you means you're stuck.

But no. Staying power is a Kingdom principle.

It's Noah building for decades with no rain.

It's Ruth gathering scraps before the harvest.

It's you showing up in your business, honoring what God said, even when the results don't yet match the promise.

Obedience isn't just a launchpad. It's the daily grind, the slow burn, the small faith steps repeated until they become a lifestyle.

Psalm 37:3 says, "Trust in the Lord and do good; dwell in the land and cultivate faithfulness."

That's a business strategy most marketing gurus won't teach, but it works.

What God Builds, He Sustains

Here's the beautiful thing: When you let God be the architect, you don't have to worry about keeping the house standing.

You don't have to overextend, overprove, or overcompensate.

Yes, you'll still do the work. But it's not just your effort keeping things alive, it's grace, multiplied.

When you've built something with God, it doesn't fall apart just because one launch underperforms. It's sustained through prayer, wise stewardship, strategic rest, and faithful work. That's the foundation you're now standing on.

The Ripple Effect of Your 'Yes'

You may never know how your obedience impacted others. Maybe you stayed faithful when others quit. Maybe you showed what it looks like to build with integrity. Maybe you gave another woman permission to trust God with her dream, too.

Remember, people are always watching, especially your children, your friends, and your clients.

Your obedience has ripple effects you won't always see.

2 Corinthians 9:13 reminds us, "Because of the service by which you have proved yourselves, others will praise God."

Your obedience is a testimony in motion.

Obedience is the Strategy

Let me say it again for the woman still wrestling with doubt:

Obedience is the strategy.

Yes, you can optimize your funnel.

Yes, you can tweak your packages.

Yes, you can upgrade your website.

But if God isn't in it, it won't last.

The strategy that brings peace, provision, and purpose always starts with obedience.

Every single time.

So if your next step feels risky but God said *Go*, do it.

And if your next step feels quiet, but God said *Stay*, do that too.

Obedience is where the harvest begins.

Reflection Questions (Let's Go Deeper)

1. Where have you been mistaking spiritual weight for failure?
2. What part of your assignment feels the heaviest right now and what if it's exactly where God is refining you?
3. Are you carrying pressure God never told you to pick up?
4. What support or structure do you need to steward your assignment without burning out?
5. How would you lead differently if you believed the weight *confirms* the call?

Chapter Summary

Obedience doesn't come wrapped in comfort. It comes with weight. Andrea doesn't sugarcoat it: When God puts a mantle on you, it *costs*. Sometimes the blessing feels like a burden. The calling feels crushing. And no one claps for the warfare behind your "yes."

But here's the shift: The heaviness isn't a sign you're doing it wrong. It's proof you're carrying something *holy*. This chapter confronts the lie that Kingdom work should be easy, and reminds you that *oil only flows from crushed olives.*

When God trusts you with something big, it won't always feel light. But it *will* be worth it.

Everything we talked about may not always be about what we think it is... In chapter 17, we'll take a look at when it is not always about the business.

It Was Never Just About the Business
(The Truth We Often Miss)

By now, you've probably realized this journey was never just about starting a business. Or making six figures. Or finally learning how to price your offers, create a budget, or manage your books without crying in the corner.

It was about becoming the woman God called you to be. The one who is no longer trying to earn approval through performance. The one who can say with holy confidence: "I am enough because He is enough."

There were days you thought about quitting. Weeks where nothing made sense. Moments when you questioned if you even heard God correctly.

And still you're here.

That alone is a testimony. Not because everything is perfect. But because you stayed in it long enough to remember why you started.

The Real Win

You may have wanted clarity. Strategy. A blueprint. A breakthrough. And maybe you got all of that. But the real win?

You stopped building from hustle and started building from healing.

You stopped treating business like your identity. And you started letting it be a tool, not a trophy.

Because let's be honest, it was never about just getting to the next income goal. It was about what God was doing in you as He walked you through each valley and victory.

You've Become Her

The woman who tithes even when it's tight because God says so.

The woman who closes her laptop early to honor her family.

The woman who no longer apologizes for being called to both business and ministry.

The woman who refuses to feel guilty about wealth because she finally understands what it means to be a Kingdom steward.

You've become her.

The Proverbs 31 woman didn't become who she was overnight. She was trusted with her home. Then her money. Then her marketplace. Then her influence.

And here you are. Trusted, tested, and still tenderhearted.

That's Kingdom business.

What Now?

This final chapter isn't the end of your story. It's just the end of this particular classroom.

You've been equipped. Not with a formula, but with faith.

Not with hype, but with holy strategy.

Not with "try harder," but with truth.

You're ready now.

Not because you've got it all figured out. But because you finally understand Who your Source is.

And spoiler alert, it's not your funnel.

So, what now?

You go back to God and ask, "What do you want to build with me next?"

And you wait.

And you listen.

And you obey.

That's the rhythm. That's the peace. That's the posture of a Kingdom woman who no longer builds from pressure but from purpose.

Final Encouragement

If there's one thing I could leave you with, it's this:

You are not behind. You are not too late. And you are not too broken.

You are right on time for God's next assignment.

Keep stewarding well.

Keep surrendering often.

Keep walking forward even when your knees shake.

And if ever you need to be reminded?

Go back to the beginning.

That mustard seed of faith. That one "yes." That quiet moment in your prayer closet where you said, "God, I'll do it if You go with me."

He did. And He still will.

This is not the end. It's the beginning of doing business in God's backyard.

Let's S.O.A.R.

Closing Prayer

"God, Help Me Build With You"

Father, thank You for walking with me through every valley and victory in this journey.

Thank You for reminding me that I was never building alone.

You have been my source when the numbers didn't make sense.

You have been my clarity when I couldn't see the next step.

You have been my peace when pressure tried to break me.

Lord, I surrender my plans, my platform, and my profits to You.

Teach me to build from alignment, not anxiety.

Help me steward what You've placed in my hands with boldness and obedience.

Strip away the guilt, the striving, the fear of failure.

Replace it with Your truth: that I am called, covered, and equipped for such a time as this.

Remind me that success in Your Kingdom isn't about being known.

It's about being faithful.

And I want to be faithful.

Let my business be a testimony.

Let my life be an offering.

And let Your name be glorified in it all.

In Jesus' name,

Amen.

From One Kingdom Builder to Another

If you've made it to this point, then I already know something about you:

You didn't just want information. You wanted transformation.

You're the kind of woman who knows that faith and business are not separate lanes.

You know that marketing doesn't have to be manipulative, that money doesn't have to be messy, and that ambition can be holy when it's submitted to God.

I didn't write this book because I had all the answers. I wrote it because I've wrestled, too.

I've cried on bathroom floors.

I've doubted my own qualifications.

I've almost quit more times than I can count.

But through every moment, God reminded me

You weren't born knowing how to do this, but you can learn with Him.

Thank you for letting me walk this part of your journey with you.

And please remember:

Your obedience is the strategy.

Your healing is the launchpad.

Your faith is the fuel.

Reflection Questions (Let's Go Deeper)

1. Where have you been demanding clarity instead of walking by faith?

2. What's one instruction God gave you that still doesn't make sense but you know it was Him?

3. Are you waiting for understanding when He's asking for action?

4. What fears are hiding behind your need to "figure it out"?

5. What would full obedience look like this week, even if the results aren't visible yet?

Chapter Summary

What do you do when God's instructions make zero sense on paper? When what He says and what you see don't match at all?

Andrea pulls no punches in this one: If you need clarity to obey, you're not walking in faith, you're walking in control. This chapter calls out our obsession with logic and invites us back into *radical trust*. Because faith won't always come with receipts. Sometimes, it comes with *contradictions*.

You'll have to walk in the dark. Move before it looks safe. Trust when the numbers say no. That's where miracles happen, not in the comfort of confirmation, but in the discomfort of obedience.

You Weren't Built to Break

If this book met you in a season where business felt like too much, it wasn't by accident. Maybe you picked this up looking for a strategy. But what do you really need? Was *permission to breathe*. To *be still*. To *belong to God more than your grind*.

You've walked through fear, fog, and frustration, and still, here you are. That's not failure. That's faith. And while the world keeps yelling, "Do more," God is whispering, "S.O.A.R."

This is your rhythm now:

S - SURRENDER

Let go of what's no longer yours to carry. Your pace. Your pressure. Your perfectionism. Surrender isn't giving up; it's giving *back* what was never meant to be your burden.

O - OBEDIENCE

Even when it doesn't make sense. Even when the metrics don't match the miracle. You weren't called to figure it all out just to say yes when God speaks.

A - ALIGNMENT

No more contorting your soul to fit a version of success God never authored. Your assignment isn't random; it's *refined*. And alignment brings the authority you've been chasing.

R - REST

You're allowed to rest. You're *commanded* to rest. Because rest is trust in action. It's how you protect your mind, your body, and your mission from burnout.

Let this book not be a period, but a pivot. A holy interruption. The moment you stopped trying to hold everything together and let God hold *you*.

You're not behind. You're just being rebuilt. You're not breaking. You're becoming.

So pause. Listen. Breathe.

Then?

S.O.A.R.

Want to keep growing? You can join the S.O.A.R.™ mentorship program, grab the workbook, or dive into our community of bold, faithless women building God's way.

If you haven't yet, be sure to check out my workbook *The S.O.A.R. Strategy Set 3 Spiritual + Strategic tools to help you heal, align and lead boldly, God's way.* It's the perfect companion to help you implement what you just read.

Visit https://thesoarstrategyset.andrearussellcoach.com/home to take the next step.

And remember, you're not behind.

You are right where God wants you to be. He is building you one day at a time.

About the Author

Andrea C. Russell is a faith-driven business coach, author, and founder of the S.O.A.R. framework for Kingdom entrepreneurs. As a mother of three who built a thriving business from scratch, Andrea knows firsthand what it's like to navigate the tension between calling and capacity, ambition and obedience, profit and peace.

Through her coaching programs, guides, courses, and now this book, Andrea helps Christian women entrepreneurs trade pressure for purpose and build businesses that honor God without breaking them. She believes that when women steward their gifts with holy confidence and humble dependence, they don't just change their lives, they change the world.

Andrea lives in Marietta GA and is passionate about family, worship, helping women of faith live a victorious life with God at the center.

Connect with Andrea at
https://businesscoach.andrearussellcoach.com/mentor
or on Instagram @christianwomenpreneur

Join The Journey

When Business Becomes Heavy

This book is more than words on a page.
It's an invitation to build your business with God, not pressure.

When Business Becomes Heavy was written for the woman who loves God, feels called to business, and is tired of carrying it all alone. If this message resonated with you, it's because you're not meant to stop here.

Ready to Go Deeper?

You don't have to figure this out by yourself.

You can continue the journey by working through the companion workbook, **From Prayers to Profits: Crafting Business in God's Backyard**, designed to help you slow down, hear God clearly, and apply what you've learned in real life.

Looking for Support and Accountability?

The **S.O.A.R. mentorship and community** were created for women just like you, women who want to grow their business without burnout, guilt, or hustle.

This is a space to learn, implement, rest, and rise, together.

Your Next Step Is Simple

You don't need more pressure.
You don't need to have it all figured out.
You just need to take the next faithful step.

Build at God's pace.
Lead with peace.
And remember, you were never meant to carry this alone.

9 781971 349176